# Contents

My Country     4

Landscape and Weather     8

At Home     10

Food and Mealtimes     14

School Day     18

Off to Work     22

Free Time     24

Religion     26

Fact File     28

Glossary     30

Further Information     31

Index     32

# My Country

Monday, 7 January

15 Paramara Street
Edapally
Kochi
Kerala
India 862173

Dear Sam,

*Namaste!* (This means 'hello' in Hindi.)

My name is Lakshmi Menon and I'm 9 years old. I live in Kochi, on the coast of Kerala, in India. Look on the map to see where Kochi and Kerala are. Being your pen-pal is a great idea – I'll be able to help you with class projects on India.

Write back soon!

From

## Lakshmi

Here I am with Dad, Mum and my brother, Nithin – he's 11 years old.

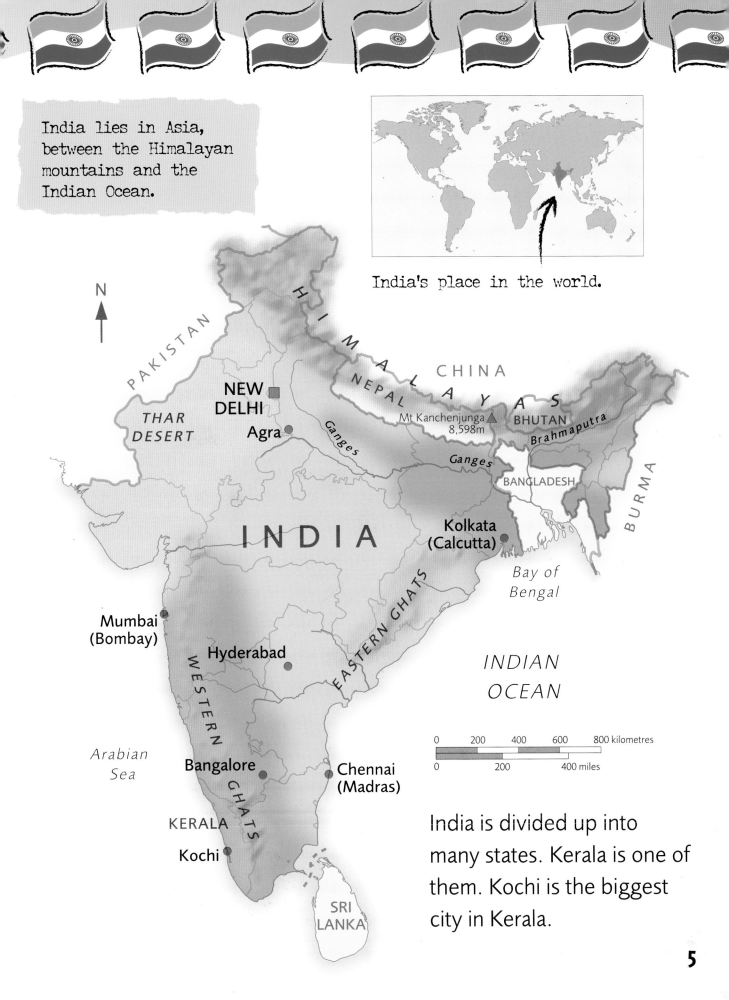

India lies in Asia, between the Himalayan mountains and the Indian Ocean.

India's place in the world.

N

PAKISTAN

THAR DESERT

NEW DELHI

Agra

HIMALAYAS

NEPAL

CHINA

Mt Kanchenjunga 8,598m

BHUTAN

Brahmaputra

Ganges

Ganges

BANGLADESH

BURMA

INDIA

Kolkata (Calcutta)

Bay of Bengal

Mumbai (Bombay)

Hyderabad

WESTERN GHATS

EASTERN GHATS

INDIAN OCEAN

Arabian Sea

Bangalore

Chennai (Madras)

| 0 | 200 | 400 | 600 | 800 kilometres |
| 0 | | 200 | | 400 miles |

KERALA

Kochi

SRI LANKA

India is divided up into many states. Kerala is one of them. Kochi is the biggest city in Kerala.

Kochi is a very busy place. About 800,000 people live there. Kochi is the most important city in Kerala because it has a large port. Ships from all over the world take away coir, rubber, tea and spices from Kerala.

Like most Indian cities, Kochi's streets are always busy with traffic.

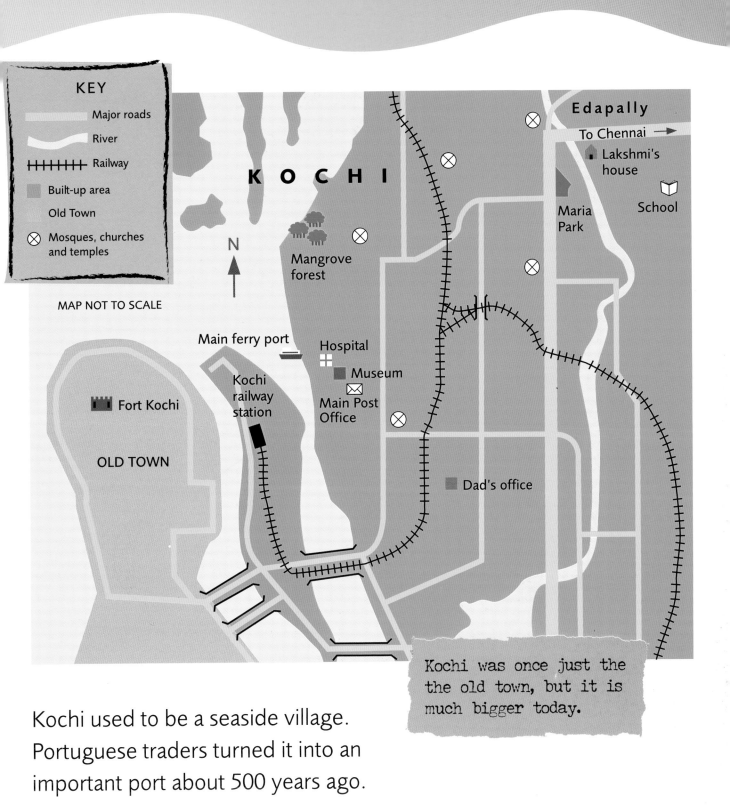

KEY

Major roads

River

Railway

Built-up area

Old Town

⊗ Mosques, churches and temples

MAP NOT TO SCALE

N

**K O C H I**

Mangrove forest

Main ferry port

Hospital

Museum

Kochi railway station

Main Post Office

Fort Kochi

OLD TOWN

Dad's office

**Edapally**

To Chennai →

Lakshmi's house

School

Maria Park

Kochi was once just the the old town, but it is much bigger today.

Kochi used to be a seaside village. Portuguese traders turned it into an important port about 500 years ago.

Lakshmi lives in an area called Edapally, in north-east Kochi. Once it was a separate village. But the city of Kochi has grown so much that Edapally is now part of it.

7

# Landscape and Weather

Kerala is squeezed between hills, called the Western Ghats, and the Arabian Sea. It is criss-crossed by many rivers flowing down from the hills into the sea.

Kerala is very flat and full of trees. Bridges have been built to cross its many rivers.

North India has high mountains and a big desert. The mountains are cold and wet. The desert is hot and dry. Kochi is hot all year round. A wind called the monsoon brings a lot of rain between May and October.

## Kochi's Climate

| January | July |
|---|---|
| Temperature | Temperature |
| 27°C | 26°C |
| 10mm Rainfall | 572mm Rainfall |

Lakshmi often needs an umbrella to keep dry during the rainy season.

# At Home

Lakshmi lives in a house that was built four years ago by her parents. Her Grandma Kochammini lives there, too. Lakshmi's other grandparents, Grandad Achuthan and Grandma Indira, live just around the corner.

Grandma Kochammini has lived with Lakshmi's family since her husband died.

This is Lakshmi with her mum and brother, Nithin, in front of their house.

When the Menon family moved here many years ago there were few houses. Today there are homes everywhere. There is no empty land left on which to build any new buildings.

Lakshmi in her bedroom. She shares this room with Nithin.

Lakshmi and her friends like to play outside in the front yard.

Lakshmi's house has two floors. On the ground floor there are two lounges, a kitchen, a dining-room and Grandma Kochammini's room.

Upstairs there are two bedrooms, each with its own bathroom, and a study.

This is Lakshmi's dog, Jackie. She lives in a big kennel outside.

Tuesday, 12 March

15 Paramara Street
Edapally
Kochi
Kerala
India 862173

Dear Sam,

Thanks for your letter which arrived last week. Have I told you about Grandma Kochammini? She lives with us. Most families in India have a relation living with them. Do your grandparents live with you? Grandma Kochammini has food ready for us when we get back from school, starving! She's teaching me how to cook. I might send you a recipe next time.

From

# Lakshmi

Here I am helping Grandma Kochammini cook a meal.

# Food and Mealtimes

Lakshmi begins her day at 6 a.m. with a *dosa*, a kind of pancake, for breakfast. Sometimes she also has an *idli*. This is a sticky ball of rice that is eaten with a bowl of *sambar*, a vegetable soup with tamarind spice. For lunch Lakshmi has rice and curried vegetables, or sandwiches.

Lakshmi helps Grandad Achuthan buy some fresh vegetables at the local market.

India's climate is hot enough to grow bananas. This banana tree is in Lakshmi's garden.

At about 7.30 p.m. she eats *chapattis* or *dosas* and a potato or vegetable curry for dinner. The Menons do not eat meat, and most of their food is fresh.

The Menon family has *dosas* for dinner.

Friday, 2 May

15 Paramara Street
Edapally
Kochi
Kerala

Hi Sam!

India 862173

I promised I'd send you a recipe – here's how to make *dosas* :

You will need:  295g long-grain rice,  75g *urad dhal*, water,
$1/2$ teaspoon fenugreek spice,  pinch of salt,  vegetable oil

1. Soak the rice in a bowl of water for 8 hours, and soak the *urad dhal* in another bowl of water.
2. Drain the rice and grind it in a blender for 3 minutes, then stir in 4 tablespoons of water to make a smooth paste.
3. Drain the *urad dhal* and grind it in the blender for 5 minutes with the fenugreek. Stir in 4 tablespoons of water to form a paste.
4. Mix the rice and *urad dhal* paste together and add the salt.

I'm checking the mixture's thickness here.

5. Cover and leave for 12 hours. (The mixture should double in size.)

6. Grease a griddle pan and heat it up. Spoon enough of the mixture on to the pan to cover it.

The dosa mixture hardens in the griddle pan.

7. When the batter has thickened, dribble some oil on to it and then flip it over. (Mum always does that bit for me.)

8. In 2 minutes the *dosa* is ready to eat.

Try them and let me know what you think.

# Lakshmi

Two dosas ready for eating – delicious!

# School Day

This is Lakshmi's school bus.

Lakshmi and Nithin go to the Vidyodaya School, which is about 8 kilometres away from Edapally. Most of the pupils use the school's buses to get there. They pick up children from all over Kochi. Lakshmi catches a bus every morning at 7.20 a.m.

There are 27 children in Lakshmi's class.

Most schools in India are state schools and are free. The Vidyodaya School is a private school so Lakshmi's mum and dad pay for her and Nithin to study there.

These children go to another school in Kochi. They travel there in an auto-rickshaw.

Lakshmi's school library
has books in Hindi,
India's main language,
and other languages.

The school year begins in June and ends in March.
Then there is a long holiday in April and May.
Children begin school when they are 6 years old.
They leave when they are 17 to go to
college or university.

These boys are
practising for the
school basketball team.

Wednesday, 17 July

15 Paramara Street
Edapally
Kochi
Kerala
India 862173

Hi Sam,

Thanks for your last letter. You wanted to know what I do at school. This is what happened today:

8.00–8.30 a.m. Assembly
8.30–9.25 a.m. Science
Break
9.30–10.30 a.m. Maths
10.30–11.30 a.m. English
Lunch

12.00–12.40 p.m. Singing
12.40–1.25 p.m. Mallayalam
(Kerala's language)
Break
1.30–2.10 p.m. Games
2.10–2.50 p.m. Hindi
Home time!

My favourite lesson is Science because we learn such interesting things with our teacher. What's yours?

From

# Lakshmi

My teacher plays a harmonium in our singing lessons.

# Off to Work

Lakshmi's mum teaches English at the Vidyodaya School. She travels on the school bus every day.

Lakshmi's dad sells medical equipment to hospitals. His office is in Kochi but he travels all over Kerala for his job. He takes the train on these trips and stays away for several days.

Lakshmi's dad at his office in the city centre.

In Kerala many things are still made by hand. This man is making furniture from bamboo.

This man earns money ironing people's clothes.

Most people in Kerala are farmers. They grow rice, coconuts, spices, fruit and vegetables on their land.

# Free Time

Sunday is the only day when the whole family is together. Lakshmi's mum and Grandma Kochammini cook a delicious meal. Lakshmi's dad plays an instrument called a harmonium. He is teaching Lakshmi to play, too.

Lakshmi often plays on the climbing frames in Maria Park, near her home.

Lakshmi likes to take her dog, Jackie, for a walk at weekends.

Nithin's favourite game is Carom. This is a traditional Indian game. It is played with counters on a board with holes at each corner. The aim is to flick the counters into the holes.

Each player has eight counters at the start of a game of Carom.

# Religion

Lakshmi prays at the shrine in her home.

Most Indian people follow Hinduism, but there are many other religions in India.

Lakshmi and her family are Hindus. They have a shrine at home where they say prayers at 6 p.m. They also visit a temple in Kochi once or twice a month.

Christians worshipping at a church near Lakshmi's home.

Friday, 6 September

15 Paramara Street
Edapally
Kochi
Kerala
India 862173

Dear Sam,

It's so exciting here at the moment – we're celebrating Onam, our harvest festival. This is the most important festival in Kerala. Everyone is on holiday and there are parties with lots of wonderful food. There will be fireworks tonight.

I wish you could see them, too!

Love

# Lakshmi

We made this pattern with flower petals outside our house for Onam.

# Fact File

**Capital city:** New Delhi. It is called 'new' because it was built specially by the British to be India's capital. It became the capital city in 1911.

**Other major cities:** The largest city in India is Mumbai (once called Bombay), followed by Kolkata (Calcutta). Chennai (Madras) and Hyderábád are also large cities.

**Neighbouring countries:** Pakistan, Nepal, Bhutan, China, Bangladesh, Burma, Sri Lanka.

**Size:** 3,287,263km$^2$. India is the sixth-largest country in the world.

**Population:** 1.2 billion. India's population is the second largest in the world. (China has the largest population.)

**Languages:** Hindi and English.

**Main religions:** Hinduism is the largest religion in India. About 82 per cent of the people follow it. Islam is the next most important, with 12 per cent, and then Christianity, with 2 per cent. The rest of the people follow religions such as Sikhism, Buddhism and Jainism.

**Flag:** The orange stands for India's Hindu people. The green stands for its Muslims. The white in between stands for the hope that the Hindus and Muslims can live together happily. The wheel in the centre is an old symbol for peaceful change.

**Currency:** Indian rupee (divided into paise. 100 paise=1 rupee). Indian notes often have a picture of Mahatma Gandhi on one side.

**Main industries:** Iron and steel, clothing, jewellery, handicrafts.

**Highest mountain:** Kanchenjunga (8,598m) is in north-eastern India. It is the third-highest mountain in the world.

**Famous buildings:** The Taj Mahal in Agra is one of the world's most beautiful buildings. It was built by the Emperor Shah Jahan in memory of his wife, Mumtaz Mahal. It took 17 years to build and was finished in 1653.

**Longest river:** The River Ganges (2,655km). Hindus believe that the Ganges is a holy river, so it is very special to them. They say that bathing in it brings them good luck.

**Famous people:** Mahatma Gandhi was born in 1869. He is known as the 'Father of the Nation' because he helped India to become independent from British rule. He was killed in 1948.

**Stamps:** Ordinary stamps in India have a picture of Mahatma Gandhi on them. Some stamps celebrate different parts of Indian life. These stamps show some of its wildlife.

# Glossary

**curried** Food that has been flavoured with many spices.

*chapatti* Circular flat bread, a bit like a thick pancake.

**coir** Coconut fibres, used to make ropes and sacks.

*dosa* A thin pancake made from rice or lentils.

**harmonium** A musical instrument with a keyboard, which the player pumps with air.

**Hindi** The most important language in India.

*idli* A sticky ball of food made from ground-up rice.

**monsoon** The name of the wind that blows over India from the Arabian Sea. It brings a lot of rain.

**Onam** The most important festival in Kerala. It celebrates the end of the harvest.

**private school** A school where parents have to pay for their children to study.

*sambar* A clear soup made from vegetables and lentils.

**shrine** A sacred place. It can be a building or a special area inside a home.

**spice** Something that is used to give food a flavour.

**state** An area within a country which is like a 'mini-country'.

**tamarind** A fruit with a sour taste.

**temple** A building in which people pray.

*urad dhal* A type of lentil, found in most good supermarkets. To make dosas, you could use any type of lentil.

# Further Information

## Information books:

*Celebrate: India* by Robyn Hardyman (Franklin Watts, 2009)

*Countries in the News: India* by Anita Ganeri (Franklin Watts, 2009)

*Country Insights: India* by David Cumming (Wayland, 2008)

*Destination Detectives: India* by Anita Roy (Raintree, 2006)

*Families and Their Faiths: Sikhism in India* by Bruce Campbell (Cherrytree Books, 2009)

*Food Around the Word: India* by Polly Goodman (Wayland, 2009)

*Popcorn Countries: India* by Ruth Thomson (Wayland, 2010)

*Geeta's Day* by Prodeepta Das (Frances Lincoln, 2003)

*Prita Goes to India* by Prodeepta Das (Frances Lincoln, 2007)

*Children Around the World: We Live in India* by Philippe Godard (Harry N. Abrams, 2006)

*A Visit To India* by Peter & Connie Roop (Heinemann Library, 2008)

*A World of Food: India* by Anita Ganeri (Franklin Watts, 2010)

## Fiction:

*Chanda and The Mirror of Moonlight* by Margaret Bateson Hill (Evans, 2008)

*Lighting a Lamp: A Divali Story* by Jonny Zucker (Frances Lincoln, 2005)

*Rama and the Demon King* by Jessica Souhami (Frances Lincoln, 2005)

*Stories from Ancient Civilisations: Indian Myths* by Shahrukh Husain (Evans, 2008)

# Index

Numbers in **bold** refer to photographs and illustrations.

buildings 11
  Taj Mahal **29**

cities
  Chennai **5**, 28
  Kochi 4, **5**, **6**, **7**, 8,
    18,19, 22, 26
  Kolkata **5**, 28
  Mumbai **5**, 28
  New Delhi **5**, 28

family **4**, **10**, **11**, 12,
  **13**, **14**, **15**, **17**,
  **22**, 24
farming 23
festivals 27
  Onam **27**
flag **28**
food **13**, **14–17**, 24
  *chapattis* 15
  curried vegetables
    14, 15
  *dosas* 14, **15**, 16

*idli* 14
rice 14, 16, 23
*sambar* 14
spices 6, 14, 16, 23
tea 6
*urad dhal* 16
free time **24–25**

games 25
Gandhi, Mahatma 29

homes **10–13**

Kerala 4, **5**, 6, 8, 22, 23,
  27

languages 4, 20, 21,
  22, 28

market **14**
monsoon 8
mountains 8, 29
  Kanchenjunga **5**, 29
music **21**, 24

pets **12**, **25**
population 28

religion **26–27**, 28
  Christianity **26**
  Hinduism **26**
rivers **8**, 29
  Ganges **5**, **29**
rubber 6

school 13, **18–21**

transport 18, 19, 22
  auto-rickshaws **19**
  buses **18**, 22
  ships 6
  trains 22

weather 8, **9**, 15
Western Ghats **5**, 8
work **22–23**